The Other Side of the Mirror

D1515949

Alanna Lea Wiest

chipmunkapublishing
the mental health publisher

Published by
Chipmunkapublishing
PO Box 6872
Brentwood
Essex CM13 1ZT
United Kingdom

http://www.chipmunkapublishing.com

Chipmunkapublishing gratefully acknowledge the support of Arts Council England.

Author Biography

Alanna was born on Long Island, New York in 1976. She has lived in New York, England, Ireland, Scotland and Austria. She is a passionate equestrienne, professional artist and writer.

When Alanna was fifteen she was hospitalized for the first time for self-mutilation, suicidal ideation and depression. She was very delusional about people and situations, it was only much later when she was taking anti-psychotic medications that her thoughts cleared. At this time she was still in private school and also competing every week at major horse shows (rather dangerous and scary now that she recalls).

What has followed is over twenty five hospitalizations, numerous medicine changes and the bogeyman of all treatments ECT.

She learned early on that it was up to her to educate herself in all facets of this disease, schizoaffective disorder, to find humor where and when she can . (If someone asks her "did you hear that.?" She says don't ask me). She is very pro-active in educating and advocating for those with mental illness. She has spoken to college classes and also medical staff in hospitals.

For several years Alanna saw Dr. Martin Roshco of Huntington, New York. She credits Dr. Roshco and Dr. Jeremy D. Coplan with being a source of constant support. Alanna has been seeing Dr. Coplan for the past several years. He has always encouraged her artistic efforts and has created a very special bond.

At present Alanna is on a huge menu of medications but she is self-employed, training horses and riders. She is also a professional artist who has had six shows in Manhattan galleries and thirty gallery shows on Long Island .

Alanna hopes to reach people's emotions and lives through her poetry.

The cover is one of Alanna's paintings "Pas de Deux, Deux Danceurs" acrylic

The Other Side of the Mirror

Foreword by Jeremy D. Coplan, M.D.

Professor of Psychiatry at SUNY-Downstate Medical Center

Alanna Wiest has been under my care for the last fifteen years while struggling with the tormenting symptoms of Schizoaffective Disorder. However, as this volume of poetry attests, Alanna has put every ounce of effort into not giving in an inch. I have developed a profound admiration for her courage, as she continues to excel in her writing of poetry, painting and exhibiting her works, doing crafts such as knitting and weaving and training student horse riders and caring for horses. Moreover she has qualified as a veterinary assistant.

This impressive list of accomplishments is accentuated through a reading of her poetry. Alanna displays an extraordinary gift of penetrating deep into the soul of one who has sublimated the internal fight to survive her illness.

This prolific volume will provide an unusual voyage into the disappointments and victories of Alanna's life.

November 30, 2009
Brooklyn, New York

Alanna Lea Wiest

A DARK MIRROR

Looking through a dark mirror
Never seeing my face
Only shadows of light
Looking for something strong
Looking for something real
But nothing can be seen
I long and lust for something there
Yet nothing does appear
Black and gray is all I see
No reflection is there
Nothing but darkness.
I wish to see,
To keep me going
Something strong.
I need to be here
Looking into that dark mirror
To keep me sane and safe.

A DROP OF RAIN

A drop of rain
On this parched land
Needing the moisture
Dreaming of wet
Spring will come soon
Then all will be lush
The leaves will prosper
In this world of ours
Soon the flowers will come
Beauty will be renewed on earth
All we will see
Is all we can love
Soon winter will leave
Life will awaken.

AFRAID

Afraid of what's to come
Will she be ok?
Can't tell him yet
Though I truly ache to do so
So sweet and innocent
Why is this happening to her?
I cry a tear
But that will not help
Strength is what she needs
For him it's harder
She's been through it before
Will the outcome be worse in the future?
Why is this happening to her?

AGAINST THE WALL

Against the wall
My soul is stuck
Never to be whole again
I can not see
I can not feel
Overpowered by this thing
That we call life
A sea of pain
The land of fear
An air of nothingness
Lack of any feeling
Avoid in my brain
Not knowing what to say
Not knowing what to do
How will this end?
What can I do?

ANGER

Will he be mad, angry suppose?
I can cry
Yet the tears run dry
I could scream
Yet no noise or sound
I smile now because he doesn't know
No suspecting, it's the way to go
Please tell no one.

ANXIETY

A prisoner in my own mind
Thoughts racing all over
Crippled by my ideas
Struggling to breathe
Yet the air is so stiff
Choking with each gasp
Life is flashing sharply
Right behind my eyes
The reason is crippling
The pain lies deeper
How can I reach them?
Who can I trust?
One more time
One more fear.

APPREHENSION

A little apprehension
Afraid these feelings will end
I want so much
To be calm and well
Yet a storm lingers in the shadows
Blue sky please be here
I know the sun won't always shine
Cloudy days will come
But hopefully the blackness will cease
The light will prevail and try to stay forever.

A PUZZLE

Waiting never seemed so long
The hours are deadly
Looking for a bright future
Wanting peace
Shades of this happen
Yet it always returns
Nothing looks real
Nothing
A puzzle needing to be solved
But the pieces don't always fit
Like a painting
With undrying paint
Or a maze with no escape
Waiting never seemed so long
But what am I waiting for?

A WEAPON

Pain known as a weapon
A blade of fear
A match lit in time
Suffering so clear
To all that know me
This is a challenge
Something to be revered
So close to the pain
Happiness so far away
Ecstasy mixed with hate
Loving mixed with torture
Can we go on?
Or is this how life will end?

BEAUTY OF LIFE

I am so lucky to feel such soul
I don't take this bliss for granted
The beauty of life is so clear
I can say I love this life I live
At times the glass fogs over and then I forget
But each day I become stronger
I can truly say I've learned so much
The experiences have made me who I am
I wouldn't trade it for anything
So today I can say I'm truly happy
And in this life that's all that matters
To live this life to it's fullness and enjoy every moment
Each day proves my strength
As I said before, I wouldn't trade it for anything.

BONES

The storm is coming,
I can feel it in my bones,
Torturing my brain,
Killing my soul,
Draining my body of life
Loud screams haunt me,
Yet silence is sharp,
Nothing looks real,
As if I'm not there
Not grounded in this place
No emotions to be explained
Afraid of what's to come
The future seems so dark
Maybe, just maybe it will clear?
The storm is coming,
Yet the sky looks brighter already.

CAROUSEL OF LIFE

Carousel of life
Round and round it goes
Back and forth
Rotating this way for hours
My mind works the same way
Never stopping
Not even for a breath
Spinning with crazy thoughts
Boggling my mind
Sanity eludes me
The thrill will be next
Then the bottom falls out
Depression so strong
Could even last for months
But then again
The high is here
Faster this time
So full of joy
I feel I can do anything
I know that's true
Just pray it stays
But I know it won't.

CONTROL

I need control
But can never have it
I need a life
Yet it'll never be
Under this constant war
Never a calm in the storm
Like a wave in the ocean
Always moving this way or that
This craziness will never stop
Hearing, seeing, tasting, smelling
What is real?
And what is not?
How do I know?
No one can explain
Unless you've experienced it
Unless this is you
So let it be without control.

COLORS

The colors of life
Shades of blue and green
The sharpness of red
Feelings of black
The yearning of yellow
My soul can not choose
A rainbow of emotions
The darkness of night
The brightness at dawn
Swirling around in my brain
Total confusion is here
How long will this go on?
Fearing it's forever
Longing for it to go
Yet praying for it to stay
The colors of life in my mind.

DADDY'S LITTLE GIRL

Every little hug,
Every helping hand,
Means so very much-
I hope you know how much I care,
I may not show it every day-
But in my heart you'll always stay.
Someone to look up to-
Someone to revere-
I'm still daddy's little girl
No matter how I appear
Through times of heartache
And times of joy
You're always there for me
I really hope through these few words,
You can truly see
How much I care for and love you
How much you mean to me.

DEEPER

Deeper and deeper into darkness of madness
My soul and mind slip away
If only for a minute, a second, an hour
Trying and massacring my small little brain
Teasing, yelling, screaming, cursing at me
Will they ever cease?
Are they real?
Is it my mind?
Like a cat, I stalk the dark night
Preying on what I can find
Leave me, please don't
Alone is how I feel
In a crowd or in solitary
The thoughts make no sense
Will they know?
Will they find out?
What will happen then?
My soul will wilt like a rose in the fall
The end will never be too close
Yet I need to live
I need the help
But the hell is always so strong
Does this make sense?
To me it does
But to others I seem insane.

DELUSIONS

I know I can do it
I know I can
It's all a state of mind.
Concentrating
Willing
Thinking
The pool balls move
The phone rings
People's quiet thoughts
I can control them
I know I can
I tell no one
I don't need to
It's just the way it is
Once again I concentrate
I just need to think
Is this a test?
Of my strength
Of my body
Of my soul.

DREAMING

Sleeping so soundly
Dreaming so sweet
Hours of joy and comfort
Praying not to wake
Swirling around
These wonderful things
Deep into ecstasy
The dream does not stay long
The world does not move
Nothing bad survives
To keep the joy
Over and over again.

DREAMS

Life is just a dream,
In which one never wakens.
Pain, happiness, despair and hope,
The common man has no grasp.
This life we live,
Each day goes by,
Reality is still unclear.
Fantasy rules the life of many a man,
We must face up to the truth.
The truth is the only way to be free,
Free from your own self - destruction.

DRIPS DOWN

The candle is lit
Slowly the wax drips down
Blood red and hot
Burning to the end
Soon life will be over
Never to breathe again.
Like life itself
Pain and suffering are in the air.
A tear so very far away
Going insane
Losing its mind.
Smaller and smaller
Burning to the end
Life is now over
Nothing more to do.

EACH DAY

Each day goes round
Just like this circle
They tell me to listen
That I will get hurt
People are watching me
Plotting against me
They can read my mind
At this point I neglect
The feelings to hurt my self
I feel so alone
Alone is how I feel in this world of confusion
Every thing seems so hard
I'm afraid to even leave my bed
I can hear their thoughts
The man who's trying to kill me is no longer here
That helps a bit
All this damn noise is so loud
My brain is in turmoil
I just can't deal with it
I understand the signs.

ECT

Waking up early
I know what's to come
Afraid of what's to happen
The shot
The IV
Slowly I drift off
Next I know
I'm waking
My head hurts
I am stiff
Everything foggy
Next I know
I'm sleeping
Tomorrow it will happen
All once again
The headache
The stiffness
The confusion.

EVERY SECOND

Each day of painful life-
Thankfully is a sooner day to demise.
Every second lived, passes ever so slowly.
In this wretched reality which comes before us,
There is never a true escape.
Trying in any way to get relief from the agony-
Only accused of wrong doings,
Then sentenced for the crime.
Not knowing what to do next,
You give unto their way of life,
Finding later the pain to return again and again.

FALL

The leaves are so beautiful
All shades of yellow, orange and red
They fall to the ground
A sea of beauty
Blowing in the wind
Their majestic dance
The wind plays the music
This stunning ballet.

FEAR

My system is shutting down
Arms and legs not moving
I can't feel my fingers
Can't catch my breath
Afraid of what's happening
Afraid of what's to come
My toes feel numb
My brain is foggy
Is death near?
Or will this pass?
I am so frightened.
What shall I do?
What can I do?

FEELING REAL

Nothing feels very real
Drifting above reality
Grounding is not in my mind
The day goes so slow
Yet time is so fast
Understanding is far from me
Let me out of this mental hell
When will the symptoms cease?
Hearing, seeing, feeling not quite real
In a different realm I wade
A closer to be
Waiting
Forever can not come too soon.

FEELINGS

This hex bestowed upon my soul,
These feelings never cease.
From this nightmare I shall not wake,
Until the very end.
Each day drags on,
Each night is long,
As pain controls my life.
Every breath I take,
Is closer to the end.
This life was meant to demise.

FIRE

In the fire
I see so much.
Faces -
Creatures -
Dancing back n' forth
Are they really there?
Or is it in my mind
I envision so much
Is it real?
My mind works in overdrive
Racing all over the place
The visions are so clear
So crisp
So precise
So definite
The flicker of light
So hot
So beautiful
I feel it now
I'll feel it forever.

FLOWER

Each flower that blooms
Each tree that turns
It's just a show of joy in the world
If you're not happy it's not worth it
We need to live in beauty
Like the waves in the ocean
Like a beautiful clear sky
Happiness is what's important.

FLYING HIGH

Flying so high
Barely touching the ground
Ecstasy ! Euphoria !
All so inviting
Thoughts so fast
Thoughts so clear
What will happen next?
Not wanting to come down
This state is so great !
Like I said
What will happen next?
Round and round
My mind works too fast
Quicker, quicker
More speed enhanced
Brilliant yet insane
Which will it be?
Can't stay focused
To finish this.
Maybe in time.

FOND MEMORIES

Fond memories as far away
But good as I remember
A change in time
A long time ago
Following me in life
Flowing like a river
Flying in the sky
A drop of rain
Even when it dries
The imprint is there
Never to be lost
Love is in the air.

FOOT STEPS

Foot steps on the roof
Ghosts in the walls
Demons under foot
I hear the screaming
The crying
The panting
Afraid for my life
The water runs alone
The sleep never in the bed
The stairs lead to hell
This house is possessed
I live in this crazy world
There is no answer
Only for a few.

FOREVER

To hear the voices
Come and go
The feelings of joy hardly show
When I'm surrounded by this evil beast
Who feeds upon my soul and mind
If only I could have some time
Without a care or worry
This happiness I feel right now
Is total bliss to me
I just wish it would last
For I know I've earned it, plus more
I'd love to feel this way forever.

FRENZY

This frenzy
As my life goes
Too confusing to most
Yet sane for me
Round and round the thoughts race
Taking over my mind
Every idea is crowded
Every emotion is spent
This goes on and on
More intense by the minute
Yet so much fun
This high is from no drug
This elation has no excuses
Just let me keep enjoying
For soon it will be over.

HATRED

This hatred I know so well-
From wounds so deeply scarred,
Singled out like innocent prey,
Caught in a web of pain.
Blinded by my own despair,
Hearing only agonizing screams.

HEARING

I can hear the air
And see the sound
Senses so sharp and loud
The end will be soon
Awakening each morning
Everything so very bleak
God damn all the noise going on in my brain
Calling me closer
The end is near
No one believes me
I can hear what they're saying
All the words hurtful
I know what their saying
No one believes me
I'm all alone.
I can hear the air
And see the sound.

HEART BEAT

The heart beat so silent-
Yet its presence intrudes.
This peace I could be in,
If this beat would just stop.
Each day I wait for the drum to cease,
I wonder if my wish will come true.
The cessation of this beat would please my soul.
The truth is yet so painful.

HELLO

"Hello", Are you really there?
Or is it in my mind?
So loud, so loud
This noise penetrating my brain
Senses so sharp
To see I need to touch
To feel I need to see
Apart from myself
I don't understand
What is going on?
I cry a bit but not in pain
I don't know what the future has in store?
Which frightens me immensely
To a degree I feel no more.

The Other Side of the Mirror

HIM

The man I loved
Is not him
Further away each day
The lies
The deceit
Never kind anymore
Never loving
I gave myself to him
Body, mind and soul
Why did this happen?
How could I not know?
The future is so bleak
I must get out
Leaving him is the only way
My heart is breaking
But it's what I must do
To save myself
Not to go insane.

HOW DID I KNOW

How did I know,
What I should I do
What was meant to happen
What was meant to be
Wishing and wishing
The tide would go out
The summer turns to fall
The snow would melt
These fears go away
How will I know
The craziness is here
Screams coming from above
Yelling in the air
A peace is in the distance
A void needing to be filled
How it is now
Fear overcomes me
This is the way it'll be.

HURT

No more hospitals
No thoughts of self harm
Neither down or high
Just afraid of the outcome
What is the solution?
The answers, what will it be?
I must stop now
This poem has its end.

I HEAR THEM

My breath is lost
Far from my body
Each touch
So long away
Dripping this emotion
Possessing my thoughts.
I hear them running
Through the walls
I hear them screaming
In the air
So loud, so loud
Never quiet again
Is peace never?
Oh! Will this never end.

INTERRUPTIONS

In my life
There were many interruptions
Younger it was pain
Older it was more
My life has changed
Hardly ever a calm
Not achieving
As much as I could
Almost stopping my life
Plans unfulfilled
Wishes never coming
Goals washed away
Like the tide in the spring
Disappointing till nothing's left
Draining me of sanity
Letting go
I must accept this
But I won't give up.

INVISIBLE

To me I can't see it
Yet I know it is there
Pain
Love
Hate
Suffering
All emotions at once
Lacking any feeling
A void in my brain
Swallowing my existence
Leaving nothing behind
What to look forward to
What should I hide?
Is there any shame?
To living this life
The way I must
The only way to survive
Darkness taking over
No light to be shed
Invisible to me
For I can not see
All that is hidden
Will now be exposed.

JAMES

Round and round the tank I swim
Colorful rocks on the floor
A plant or two
A little castle to circle
Not that much to do
Oh! The food has come
I bubble up to the top
Maybe soon I'll get a friend
That would be nice
The cat sits waiting
Wanting to catch me
But never fear
She doesn't like water
So I just swim
And be happy.

KITTY

She hears a mouse
It's in the wall
She knows it's there
Waiting and waiting
For it to come out.
This cat stalks all night.
Whiskers at attention
A paw ready to strike
She likes the hunt
Up for a challenge
Ready to pounce
Loving the game
The mouse sleeps
She gets bored
Curls into a ball
And falls asleep.

LIES

The lies all come out now
Too many stories to be told
Afraid of their thoughts and judgments
Not wanting to disappoint them
What will they think?
Will it be less of me?
Ashamed in a way
Yet scared to let them know.

LOVE

What is love?
Is it something you can see, taste or smell?
Is it something you're born knowing?
Or is learned?
Is pain part of it?
Or is it something else?
I love as much as I can
Yet shadows lurk so softly
He doesn't mean to hurt me
Though times he does
I wonder if he feels the same.
I give him my all
Does it mean as much?
In prayer I submerge
Only asking for respect, kindness, and equality
Oh please be there for me
For I am here for you.

LOVERS

Lovers intertwine
Like a wave crashing upon the rocks,
The kiss so sensuous
The touch so deep
They fulfill each other's dreams,
Passing through night and day.
They long for each other.
Their love will always be.
A laugh,
A smile.
What more can they want?
Looking into each other's eyes
They were meant for each other
In times apart she longs for him
His thoughts of her
Of love
Of lust
To be together enriches their souls
They belong together forever.

NO

Hearing noises
Yet no sound
Seeing things
Yet no light
Feelings of terror
Flashing thru my mind
What shall I do?
What can I do?
They're after me
But no one's there
What have I done wrong?
In this life I lead
Do I deserve
Suffering over the years?
Will peace come?
Or will it just end?

NOISE

The music is so loud and clear
But brings the tears oh so near
A single voice or lots of noise
I sometimes cannot distinguish girls and boys
The pain so intense
The joy makes no sense
But there is a light without a doubt
The years flash by
Sometimes I cry
This war I will win
The fight has always been
A steep hard road
But treasures I hold
So dear and near
The future is very unclear
Yet the love I receive
Helps yet to ease
I know someday
I will be okay
For I know today is very special
Today I'm loved and that's all I need
To fight the beast
And kill his greed - Someday I will be fine.

ONE DREARY NIGHT

One dreary night,
The rain pelted,
My tears melted.
One dreary night,
The music played,
Yet no one heard.
One dreary night,
The end began,
In the light was life.
One dreary night,
Was light to shine no more.

ONE LOOK

What once looked so bleak
Now the light shows through
Each day is better and better
My mind is clear
The voices have gone
So has the fear
I look at my life
It's so full of things that make me happy
I should never again want to give up
But all feelings I shall not forget
For all of them are so real
At least while their happening
I must remember the joy and happiness
Especially when times are hard
For life is something to live in joy
Not to give in to darkness.

ONE MAJESTIC FLOWER

This one majestic flower,
Beholds such shining beauty.
The color of the petals,
Attract the sun's best rays.
In a garden among flowers,
This one angelic bloom of petals.
We look upon it as just another.
It could be gone.
We notice only for our loss,
But not for the beauty's death.
We care for only us,
Not for the beauty gone.
This one majestic flower,
Beholds such shining beauty.
The color of the petals,
Attracts the sun no more.

ONE MORE TIME

One more time is all he says
But I know it's not true
A promise broken once, is always again
I wish he wouldn't do this
Afraid for his life
Both real and surreal
When will it end?

OPEN WINDOW

The sounds so clear,
A song in itself,
Sleep sound fine creatures
For tomorrow is great.
The sun shall shine so brightly
And clouds will pass through.
Remember the creator -
And all dreams shall come true.

A prayer so clear,
Preparing for things to come.
I wish to you the best
For many moons.
And suns will shine.
The stars will come and go,
But you my friend
Will always be -
As true as fresh fallen snow.

OTHER SIDE OF THE MIRROR

Living on the other side of the mirror,
The images are all distorted.
Through virgin eyes
One only sees light
Though many tints exist.
Pain used to escape
A pleasure to some
Many look down.

PAIN

Wishing of Death,
To take this sorrow away,
To free my soul of this pain.
Pulling me further,
Down the depths of despair.
This freak that I am-
With society pushing me away,
Hiding me from most.
Making the pain worse,
Trying to make me go on-
Living in this agony.
Death is the only true cure,
But they don't want this to happen,
They want to save themselves,
From this pain.
So should I live for them!
I have till now,
But things have changed.
I need to free my soul.
It's dying in this body.
The time has come-
And it will be soon-
The end is near!

PAINFUL BREAK

Awaiting another painful break,
With a slowly mending heart,
Sensing his betrayal,
Hoping he will care,
Wanting his love,
Needing nothing more,
Slowly going insane,
Choosing only him,
Not knowing what is next.
Only thoughts she knows now-
Thoughts that read so very deep,
Letting nothing slip by.
She waits for time to pass,
Just waiting for another break.
The joy that fills me all so whole
Happiness I hold so dear.

PATIENCE

They say patience is a virtue
But they don't understand
Each step I take
Is closer to the end of time
We age as soon as we're born
The flower wilts from the bud
As a drop of rain falls
It is already drying
A snow leading to spring
I know you can listen
Yet may not understand
But this is my view
On life, time, and eternity.

PATIENCE 2

Patience I do not have
Never soon enough
I pace the halls
I count the steps
My mind goes up and down
Waiting for it to happen
Waiting for it to come
Why so eager
Can't I be happy
Can't this be enough
Needing more all the time
Faster and faster
I need it to be
Never waiting so long
I need to be early
Not to be late
This whirlwind in my mind
Will never calm again.

PEN

My hands aren't real
The pen writes itself
Fingers float on their own
The veins in my arms show through so blue
To my brain so fuzzy and mystical
A fog is coming into the shore
Everything seems so fast
Yet slow motion moves quietly
I hear the radio
Seems just too complicated
All the songs blend together
Too loud yet quiet
The watch on my wrist
I can hear it tick
Seconds and minutes seem the same
My hearing is cave like
The mist from this enters
Almost floating
My feet search for control
Nothing seems exactly real
Yet I know it's there
Things are so very interesting
But focus eludes me
Not able to concentrate
Or even have my thoughts collected
The end.

PERFECTION

Perfection is a deadly thing
Nothing is ever good enough
A canvas with no paint
A play with too few words
Always more
Never enough
A story written twenty times
Perfection is a deadly thing
For all of us involved.

PETALS

A strong petal falls
The flower cries silently
A dog walks by
Picks it up and eats it
Another petal falls
Yet time is a spiral
Running away from the people
Threatened by their presence
The flower starts to fade
To never be again
No visitor will ever know
The truly beautiful existence
No reemergence of it in full bloom
How sad
But life goes on
Ever changing
This earth we live on
Is a delicate thing.

QUIET ROOM

Prolonging the suffering
The future seems bleak
Voices yelling loudly
Fear for my life
They are coming
I can feel it in the air
Smelling the danger
Looking for help
The room is so small
Only ten steps to the wall
Sometimes seven or eight
I pace back and forth
Asking for help
Can anyone help?
The answer is no
Pain so precise
Longing for escape
Pacing and counting
There is no relief
Hungering for solution
I cannot find peace.

REMEMBERING

For all those times
I need to forget
My memory haunts me
The past is so clear
Never leaving my mind
Like a ghost in the mist
Or a wave in the sea
Pain and suffering
Madness and fear
All in one
Never a respite
Never a calm
Remembering is my curse
Never able to be blocked out
I need to forget
But I can't
All this insanity
Is there forever
My mind is scarred for life.

REPETITION

Repetition
Repetition
Repetition
My mind going crazy
Counting on and on
One, two, three, four
Tracing my steps
Five, six, seven, eight
Reviewing my words
Again and again
Over and over
I can not stop
Driven to insanity
Dropping over the edge
Diving into oblivion
Over and over
Again and again
How do I stop this?
How will this end?
Is why I'm still here.

RETURNING

Returning to the pain
Running through my head
Crazy thoughts and ideas
Climbing down this ladder to hell
The emotion
The heartache
The feelings of gloom
My life flashing in front of me
My brain in turmoil
Screams penetrating my every thought
No hope in the near future
Only insanity is next.

SHADOWS ON THE WALL

Crawling
Creeping
Running through my mind
Closing in around me
All of reality is gone
No life in the future
And nothing in the past
The walls are moving
Drifting left and right
Shadows everywhere
No escape
No rescue
Clawing at my brain
The blood runs so deep
The skin so hot
Can this be real?
I doubt it is
Yet I'm so afraid
Of what's to come
What will be
I do not know.

SINGLE FLAME

A single flame dancing through the night.
Red drops run slowly down its body.
Its life has less time remaining.
Each brings it close to death-
But it still remains silent,
Still remains peaceful.
It knows not of its life,
The flame which brings its death.

SITTING ON THE EDGE

Sitting on the edge
So far down it goes
Dropping emotions
All love and hate
When will this end?
How shall I behave?
Wind rushing through me
Entering my soul
Whipping in my heart
No peace in sight
The voices are so loud
Cutting through my thoughts
Sitting on the edge
The better is never.

SO FAR AWAY

My eyes are burning-
Yet sleep is so far away
Minutes drag in my head
The days linger on
Afraid of the future
Sad about the past
Nervousness followed
My sick little mind
Wishing calm would come
I lust for happiness
Sometimes it comes
But flees too quickly
My eyes are burning
Yet sleep is so far away.

SO LOUD

So loud- so loud
Yet noise is so low
My brain is on overdrive
Faster-faster
I deteriorate into darkness
A black hole absorbs me
Killing away sanity
What's next?
A voice, a fear, or sadness forever
Pills, pills, pills
Are they poison?
Or do they help?
They know my thoughts
I try for self control
But is that what I want?
Just extended peace.

SUMMER HAZE

A whinny from his stall
A loving nuzzle with his nose
I brush till he's clean
Which takes quite a while.
He lifts his foot
I pick his feet
The saddle goes on
Tighten his girth
Bit in his mouth
We walk together
Now to get on-
Foot in left stirrup
Then jump on
His walk is so fluid
Curled up on the bit
I ask him to trot
He tries to evade
But gives me his heart
Beauty emerges
Left leg back
We drift into the canter
He's so very strong
We move like a ballet.
I love this horse
He's answered my dreams.

SUPPORT

With everyone's agony
The lights shine dim
We need to stand together
We need the support
As hard as it may be
If we all make an effort
This day will pass
Then life will go on
The sun will shine
The rain will cry
All nature will prevail
So just take this day
To remember our losses
But pray for peace
Soon our hearts will mend
If we try we can put this day behind us
But never forget the loved ones
Who have parted from us a year ago.

SURVIVE

Driving me crazy-
They say the meds work
The shaking
The stiffness
The drugging effect
Is it really worth it?
Does it keep me well?
Does it keep me alive?
I don't know what to do
Please show me the future
Please let me know
I need to stay strong.
I need to survive.
Is this the way?
What is in store?
Things often look bleak
Help me to live
Help me stay sane.

TAKE ME NOW

Eyes so wide-
Breath so quick-
Thoughts racing-
Back and forth-
Higher n' higher-
No peak too high-
Laughing comes
So easy.
Wanting to be with you
Needing your physical passion
So excited
Please let me be happy
Please don't take euphoria away
Please take me now.

TAKE THIS-

Please take this suffering away
Help me to survive
No one takes me seriously
This pain that has become
Wanting to be well
Wishing for relief.
At the end
The light shines bright
An opening in the sky
Could this be solved?
I hope it can
I need the encouragement
I need the support
The people I love
Try so hard
Just let me not disappoint
Or shall I say "Again".

TERROR

Terror takes over
No bright light ahead
Thoughts so dim
Never understanding
The process of life
How did this happen?
Why me?
They try to help me
But the effort is pointless
I'll always be this way.

TERROR 2

Terror is all I feel
All I breathe
No escape from this hell
Down and down I fall
Reaching out for help
Yet finding no relief
Please help me
Please help me
Climb out of this place
Escape from this wretched being
Get out of this craziness
This insanity please leave
Wanting to get back this life of mine
All of what I could have been
All of what should have happened
Yet all these feelings shall be there forever.

THE DANCE

The dance just began.
They are coming
All of them
I can hear it vaguely
But each moment they are clearer
Louder more definite
To the point of scary
Round and round in my head
They tell me what to do
Evil, angelic
It's all the same
Louder now
I can't even think
Too distracting
Too overpowering
Life is so unreal
The dance continues
Until it is done
When that happens
Peace will return.

THE FALL

I enter this life
Already falling down
Blackness takes over
Bleakness envelops me
Fear of the past present and future
What has happened
What's to come
What has already been
Memories haunt me
Twisting my mind and thoughts
All the new thoughts
Louder and louder
More confusing
More frightening
Will I keep falling?
Or will I come to a stop.

THE FOG

A mist
A fog
Takes over my mind
Drowning my brain
Flooding my thoughts
No future is foreseen
No past recognized
A distant twilight
A setting sun
The moon creeping through the clouds
When dawn occurs
The fog will lift
The mist dissipate
Will I still stay this way?
Will things seem real again?

THE GIFT

The gift is given
Then taken away
Always wanting more
Never enough
Losing it is tragic
Yearning for it to stay
Most do not realize
Just how tender this is
A break in the storm
A calm in the sea
I need this to stay
I need a respite
Just looking forward
To the simple things
Like a smile
Or a positive emotion
A dove singing in the spring
A purr of a kitten
A kiss from a friendly dog
People do not realize
That these simple things
Are gifts given every day
Something to savor
Something to keep
Something to cherish forever.

THE LETTER

This letter I received
So dark in it's words
Torturing my mind
Why did he write this?
Just to cause me pain?
Just to be cruel
I need him no more
I know that in my head
The happy times are over
Bliss is all gone
I did love him
With all my heart
But that's over
Never to be again.

THE PHOTOGRAPH

Catches our souls
In memory forever
Never to be erased
A smile
A joy
A moment of happiness
There is another side
To catch someone
At evil things
They not knowing
They've been caught
Proof appears
So let it be
The next time you snap
They are in memory forever.

THE STORM

Like the wind through the trees-
My mind blows away
Rain so hard
Pelting my brain
The storm so close
Yet so far away
Shall this madness
Ever go away?
Or is this what it's all about?
Colors so bright
Yet look so dull
Thoughts whirling in my head
Never a respite from my thoughts
Haunting me
Possessing me
Trying to kill me
I won't give up
This is no simple battle
This is no peaceful war
It is my life
It is how I live
Surviving is the only choice
An uphill fight is all this is.

THE TREE

It sways in the wind,
Dancing among the flowers,
The costume swings,
As the ballet goes on.
After the dance,
It sheds its clothes,
The natural bareness,
Until redressed.
Then this tree will dance again.

THE ROSE

As if a gentle awakening,
The rain lightly pelted against the fragile rose.
To say that life is about,
And to join in on life itself.
But the rose waits,
Waits until the gentle pelting on its frail petals stop.
As the warmth of the morning sun dries the land,
The rose awakens to see all the rain had talked about.
For all the rain had left to the rose was a memory,
A memory and a single drop of water.
One drop of water that held an almost magical presence
As if the rain had wanted to be remembered,
Remembered by this beautiful young rose.

THE VOICES

Screaming and yelling
The voices never cease
Demons and angels
Tell me what to do
Danger is near
Fear of all
Nothing looks real
As if I can touch it
Yet so far away
So hyper and strung out
In the throes of sadness
The cycle never ends
Reaching for sanity
Praying for the calm
Inside of me.
I do not know
What lies ahead
In my life.

THE TEARS FALL

The tears fall
Like drops of rain
Descending to the ground
Awaiting the next storm
The clouds cease
The sun will shine
Awaiting the next day
Time goes slow
Yet time passes so very fast
The clock is right and wrong
My brain is confused
I don't know what to say
Like the storm
This stage will pass
The sky will hopefully clear.

THRILL

Seeking the thrill
Higher and higher I go
No drug can match this
No drink for effect
Spinning in wonder
So over in ecstasy
Never have I felt so good
I think I can touch the sky
The heavens have opened up
No hell is near
Soaring above the clouds
Climbing the highest peak
Nothing above me
Nothing too high
I will never come down
At least I can only hope
For seeking the thrill
Is why I'm still here.

TICK TICK TICK

Tick, tick, tick.
The clock drives my mind
Every second feels forever
Can't believe this
Never to return
Life goes by so quickly
Never time for a break
Choking the future
When will peace come?
I need to rest
I need to sleep
Yet the clock keeps going
Tick, tick, tick.

TO COME

A time when
Life was so easy
All joy and happiness
I had no worries
No sign of pain
That is long gone
So very far away
So distant every day
The sun does shine
But it never lasts
No more then a few days
Maybe a week if I'm lucky
Then the pain and torturer come back
The voices disturbing my thoughts
The pain is so intense
No escape from this hell
Waiting the week
I need it to come
To come and keep me sane
To come and not let me give up
To come and make me happy.

TORMENTED

Upon my ways.
But live my life!
And you shall feel-
Torment at its greatest
Ecstasy mixed with sorrow
Heaven with my hell.
This life I lead
Shall it ever be sane?
These emotions will they ever be gone?
I've lost my grasp of wrong and right.
My guilt like a passing storm.
The wind which blew so fierce once
Is now remembered by only few.
The last burning embers-
The last drop of rain-
One takes for granted
Every pleasure experienced.

TO THOSE

To those who raised me
And truly care
Part of them will always be with me
Those two wonderful and supportive people
I love them with all my heart
They help me day in and out
Through good and bad
They're always there for me
No matter what I say or what I do
I can count on their love
And my love for them.

TO TRY

Like a drug
Like a drink
These thoughts haunt me.
Penetrating my mind
Swirling my thoughts
I ache for a calm
I wish for a solution
Trying so hard
To escape this way
Bleakness is overpowering
Please oh Please
Let it all be okay
I don't want to end
This harsh life of mine
I know I can do it.
I just need to try.

UNSPOKEN

The words unspoken
Tells so much
No need to say out loud
Feelings experienced
My mind explores
Waiting to make sense
A fond memory
A first love
But what can I do
To savor these feelings
To keep these thoughts
Forever
The time has come
I do not know
How long this will last
If at all
Drowning in fear
Gasping for a breath
The tide takes me away
My mind goes blank
It is over
I can just feel it
Taste it
Sense it
Know it
This is the end.

WAITING

Waiting for the phone to ring
Coming through this important call
Ringing it does not
Will it soon.
Concentrating to see if it helps
My total focus
All my thoughts
Can I make this happen?
Will this wish come true?
It does not ring
Maby now it will.

WALLS OF SILENCE

Can you hear it?
Yes I do.
Faint yet loud
Strong yet soft
Angels
Demons
All the same
Surrounding my mind
Locking into my soul
Approaching madness
Leaving no prisoners
Enveloping my existence
Remembering only pain
A ghost in the fog
Shadows in the mist
An unforgettable thought
A cry for help
This wall of silence
Will never break
Wishing it away
Yet no hope is found
This is the way it is
The way it will be forever.

WAR

The war in my brain
Will it ever end?
Will the fighting ever stop?
Two sides of opposite worlds
I take two steps forward
Then one step back
So loud this internal noise
Yet silence returns
Where should I go?
What should I do?
Time just marches on.

WAVE

As a wave comes and goes
So do the voices in my head
Louder and louder the sounds connect
I am afraid
I am alone
Tortured by memories
Cursed by the future
When will it stop?
When will it end?
Spiraling down an endless path
Into the depths of darkness
My mood is good now
Neither high or down
It's the other part of my illness
That can not be controlled
A little better than yesterday
But then it happened again
Will it stop?
Will it end?

WELCOME

Welcome to my nightmare-
For now I wish to wake.
Pain so precise and so deep.
These feelings so intense,
Sickly shifted into pleasure,
Such hatred in my mind,
Wanting to hurt!
Unable to fulfill my dreams.

WHIRLWIND

Listening to silence
Feeling the untrue
Thoughts flowing crazily
A whirlwind of ideas
Do I see?
Can I taste?
Touching is a pleasure
Will this stay?
Shall the waters calm
My mind is a maelstrom
As a leaf falls in Autumn
A snowflake in the cold
Drops of rain like burning tears
What will become of me?

WHY

Why so bitchy?
It was a mistake
So judgemental
But there is needed
This nastiness is inappropriate
Why take it out on me?
I'm getting fed up
Goodbye.

WILL HE KNOW

Oh shit!
He will know
He'll find out where I am
What could be worse?
Than him showing up?
Oh why is this happening to me?
I don't ask for much
Just deal with what I have
The storm has just begun.

WRITING

Writing this poem
Takes such emotion
To bear my heart
To let out my soul
Troubles in my life
Spelled out on paper
Thoughts of pain
Thoughts of heartache
Even some thoughts of joy
The darkness looms in the distance
Coming out like a winter's dawn
Emerging like a cloud in the storm
Writing this poem
Drains my mind.

Breinigsville, PA USA
24 November 2010
249841BV00005B/2/P